I'LL NEVER TELL

KYLE KERSKIE

ISBN-13: 978-0-9832529-5-5

WHY THIS BOOK WAS CREATED

This book was created to enable you to store your passwords in a less obvious way. Our Privacy-Mentor password book series was designed to resemble an actual book. If you accidentally leave this book out on your desk, no one would suspect it contains your passwords. This book was designed to be "Hidden in Sight" on your desk or bookshelf. While we highly recommend you store this in a secure location, it was designed for those times when it's not so secure. No need to advertise on the front cover that the book contains your passwords. Might as well say "steal everything I have!" No, our books look like real books. Isn't it fun outconning the conmen?

Check out our full series of password books and more at Privacy-Mentor.com

TIPS AND TRICKS

Passwords

- Passwords should have a minimum of 12 characters.
- Think of it as a passphrase instead of a password. Use a saying, phrase, or line from your favorite book, song, or movie.
- If symbols or numbers are required, you can swap them out for letters. Here's an example: FlockofSeagulls or F!ockof$eagull5
- Passwords should be changed at least once a year **or**
    - After you believe you were involved in a data breach
    - After any incidents of fraud or identity theft

When entering a password in this book make sure you put the date next to it, so you'll know when you last updated your password.

Online Account Tier System

Now you know how long your passwords should be you might feel overwhelmed by the thought of having to change all your online account passwords. To make it easier, we've created an online account tier system. Group your online accounts into three tiers.

- Tier 1 – most important accounts
    - Financial and retirement accounts
    - Email account
    - Mobile phone carrier account
    - Work accounts
- Tier 2 – medium important accounts
    - E-commerce sites/social media
- Tier 3 – least important accounts
    - Any account that doesn't have financial or personal information linked to it such as newsletters

While all passwords should be strong, tier 1 passwords should be the strongest and, more importantly, each one unique. Tier 2 passwords should be strong, but they don't need to be as unique as your tier 1 passwords. Tier three passwords, use whatever you want. If someone breaks into it, who cares. They couldn't do any damage with the information found.

Emails

- Create a throwaway email, also known as an alias email. Use this email to avoid overloading your inbox with junk mail. Use your primary email for your important online accounts. For everything else, use an alias email address.
    - This increases the security of your email and lowers the risk of it being compromised by limiting the number of accounts it's tied to.
    - It will also help to lower the amount of spam you receive on your primary email.

Security Questions/Answers

- When answering security questions, do not your real answers. In today's digital age this information is often available for sale by data aggregators. Instead, try the "**one-off method**" and answer questions using someone you know as your answer key. For example, if I my best friend is my answer key then the answer for "my favorite movie" would be his favorite movie.
    - This prevents criminals from using any of your personal data against you.
    - You don't have to remember fake answers. You only need to remember which person is your answer key.

Two-Factor or Multi-factor Authentication

- Enable two-factor authentication (2FA) or multi-factor authentication (MFA) whenever available for your tier 1 and 2 accounts.
    - This may seem tedious sometimes, but it makes all the difference for criminals looking for vulnerabilities.

I'LL NEVER TELL

A

Website Name:
Date changed:
Email Address:
Username:
Password:
Notes:

Website Name:
Date changed:
Email Address:
Username:
Password:
Notes:

Website Name:
Date changed:
Email Address:
Username:
Password:
Notes:

A

Website Name:
Date changed:
Email Address:
Username:
Password:
Notes:

Website Name:
Date changed:
Email Address:
Username:
Password:
Notes:

Website Name:
Date changed:
Email Address:
Username:
Password:
Notes:

A

Website Name:
Date changed:
Email Address:
Username:
Password:
Notes:

Website Name:
Date changed:
Email Address:
Username:
Password:
Notes:

Website Name:
Date changed:
Email Address:
Username:
Password:
Notes:

A

Website Name:
Date changed:
Email Address:
Username:
Password:
Notes:

Website Name:
Date changed:
Email Address:
Username:
Password:
Notes:

Website Name:
Date changed:
Email Address:
Username:
Password:
Notes:

B

Website Name:
Date changed:
Email Address:
Username:
Password:
Notes:

Website Name:
Date changed:
Email Address:
Username:
Password:
Notes:

Website Name:
Date changed:
Email Address:
Username:
Password:
Notes:

B

Website Name:
Date changed:
Email Address:
Username:
Password:
Notes:

Website Name:
Date changed:
Email Address:
Username:
Password:
Notes:

Website Name:
Date changed:
Email Address:
Username:
Password:
Notes:

B

Website Name:
Date changed:
Email Address:
Username:
Password:
Notes:

Website Name:
Date changed:
Email Address:
Username:
Password:
Notes:

Website Name:
Date changed:
Email Address:
Username:
Password:
Notes:

B

Website Name:
Date changed:
Email Address:
Username:
Password:
Notes:

Website Name:
Date changed:
Email Address:
Username:
Password:
Notes:

Website Name:
Date changed:
Email Address:
Username:
Password:
Notes:

C

Website Name:
Date changed:
Email Address:
Username:
Password:
Notes:

Website Name:
Date changed:
Email Address:
Username:
Password:
Notes:

Website Name:
Date changed:
Email Address:
Username:
Password:
Notes:

C

Website Name:
Date changed:
Email Address:
Username:
Password:
Notes:

Website Name:
Date changed:
Email Address:
Username:
Password:
Notes:

Website Name:
Date changed:
Email Address:
Username:
Password:
Notes:

C

Website Name:
Date changed:
Email Address:
Username:
Password:
Notes:

Website Name:
Date changed:
Email Address:
Username:
Password:
Notes:

Website Name:
Date changed:
Email Address:
Username:
Password:
Notes:

C

Website Name:
Date changed:
Email Address:
Username:
Password:
Notes:

Website Name:
Date changed:
Email Address:
Username:
Password:
Notes:

Website Name:
Date changed:
Email Address:
Username:
Password:
Notes:

D

Website Name:
Date changed:
Email Address:
Username:
Password:
Notes:

Website Name:
Date changed:
Email Address:
Username:
Password:
Notes:

Website Name:
Date changed:
Email Address:
Username:
Password:
Notes:

D

Website Name:
Date changed:
Email Address:
Username:
Password:
Notes:

Website Name:
Date changed:
Email Address:
Username:
Password:
Notes:

Website Name:
Date changed:
Email Address:
Username:
Password:
Notes:

D

Website Name:
Date changed:
Email Address:
Username:
Password:
Notes:

Website Name:
Date changed:
Email Address:
Username:
Password:
Notes:

Website Name:
Date changed:
Email Address:
Username:
Password:
Notes:

D

Website Name:
Date changed:
Email Address:
Username:
Password:
Notes:

Website Name:
Date changed:
Email Address:
Username:
Password:
Notes:

Website Name:
Date changed:
Email Address:
Username:
Password:
Notes:

E

Website Name:
Date changed:
Email Address:
Username:
Password:
Notes:

Website Name:
Date changed:
Email Address:
Username:
Password:
Notes:

Website Name:
Date changed:
Email Address:
Username:
Password:
Notes:

E

Website Name:
Date changed:
Email Address:
Username:
Password:
Notes:

Website Name:
Date changed:
Email Address:
Username:
Password:
Notes:

Website Name:
Date changed:
Email Address:
Username:
Password:
Notes:

E

Website Name:
Date changed:
Email Address:
Username:
Password:
Notes:

Website Name:
Date changed:
Email Address:
Username:
Password:
Notes:

Website Name:
Date changed:
Email Address:
Username:
Password:
Notes:

E

Website Name:
Date changed:
Email Address:
Username:
Password:
Notes:

Website Name:
Date changed:
Email Address:
Username:
Password:
Notes:

Website Name:
Date changed:
Email Address:
Username:
Password:
Notes:

F

Website Name:
Date changed:
Email Address:
Username:
Password:
Notes:

Website Name:
Date changed:
Email Address:
Username:
Password:
Notes:

Website Name:
Date changed:
Email Address:
Username:
Password:
Notes:

F

Website Name:
Date changed:
Email Address:
Username:
Password:
Notes:

Website Name:
Date changed:
Email Address:
Username:
Password:
Notes:

Website Name:
Date changed:
Email Address:
Username:
Password:
Notes:

F

Website Name:
Date changed:
Email Address:
Username:
Password:
Notes:

Website Name:
Date changed:
Email Address:
Username:
Password:
Notes:

Website Name:
Date changed:
Email Address:
Username:
Password:
Notes:

F

Website Name:
Date changed:
Email Address:
Username:
Password:
Notes:

Website Name:
Date changed:
Email Address:
Username:
Password:
Notes:

Website Name:
Date changed:
Email Address:
Username:
Password:
Notes:

G

Website Name:
Date changed:
Email Address:
Username:
Password:
Notes:

Website Name:
Date changed:
Email Address:
Username:
Password:
Notes:

Website Name:
Date changed:
Email Address:
Username:
Password:
Notes:

G

Website Name:
Date changed:
Email Address:
Username:
Password:
Notes:

Website Name:
Date changed:
Email Address:
Username:
Password:
Notes:

Website Name:
Date changed:
Email Address:
Username:
Password:
Notes:

G

Website Name:
Date changed:
Email Address:
Username:
Password:
Notes:

Website Name:
Date changed:
Email Address:
Username:
Password:
Notes:

Website Name:
Date changed:
Email Address:
Username:
Password:
Notes:

G

Website Name:
Date changed:
Email Address:
Username:
Password:
Notes:

Website Name:
Date changed:
Email Address:
Username:
Password:
Notes:

Website Name:
Date changed:
Email Address:
Username:
Password:
Notes:

H

Website Name:
Date changed:
Email Address:
Username:
Password:
Notes:

Website Name:
Date changed:
Email Address:
Username:
Password:
Notes:

Website Name:
Date changed:
Email Address:
Username:
Password:
Notes:

H

Website Name:
Date changed:
Email Address:
Username:
Password:
Notes:

Website Name:
Date changed:
Email Address:
Username:
Password:
Notes:

Website Name:
Date changed:
Email Address:
Username:
Password:
Notes:

H

Website Name:
Date changed:
Email Address:
Username:
Password:
Notes:

Website Name:
Date changed:
Email Address:
Username:
Password:
Notes:

Website Name:
Date changed:
Email Address:
Username:
Password:
Notes:

H

Website Name:
Date changed:
Email Address:
Username:
Password:
Notes:

Website Name:
Date changed:
Email Address:
Username:
Password:
Notes:

Website Name:
Date changed:
Email Address:
Username:
Password:
Notes:

I

Website Name:
Date changed:
Email Address:
Username:
Password:
Notes:

Website Name:
Date changed:
Email Address:
Username:
Password:
Notes:

Website Name:
Date changed:
Email Address:
Username:
Password:
Notes:

I

Website Name:
Date changed:
Email Address:
Username:
Password:
Notes:

Website Name:
Date changed:
Email Address:
Username:
Password:
Notes:

Website Name:
Date changed:
Email Address:
Username:
Password:
Notes:

I

Website Name:
Date changed:
Email Address:
Username:
Password:
Notes:

Website Name:
Date changed:
Email Address:
Username:
Password:
Notes:

Website Name:
Date changed:
Email Address:
Username:
Password:
Notes:

I

Website Name:
Date changed:
Email Address:
Username:
Password:
Notes:

Website Name:
Date changed:
Email Address:
Username:
Password:
Notes:

Website Name:
Date changed:
Email Address:
Username:
Password:
Notes:

J

Website Name:
Date changed:
Email Address:
Username:
Password:
Notes:

Website Name:
Date changed:
Email Address:
Username:
Password:
Notes:

Website Name:
Date changed:
Email Address:
Username:
Password:
Notes:

J

Website Name:
Date changed:
Email Address:
Username:
Password:
Notes:

Website Name:
Date changed:
Email Address:
Username:
Password:
Notes:

Website Name:
Date changed:
Email Address:
Username:
Password:
Notes:

J

Website Name:
Date changed:
Email Address:
Username:
Password:
Notes:

Website Name:
Date changed:
Email Address:
Username:
Password:
Notes:

Website Name:
Date changed:
Email Address:
Username:
Password:
Notes:

J

Website Name:
Date changed:
Email Address:
Username:
Password:
Notes:

Website Name:
Date changed:
Email Address:
Username:
Password:
Notes:

Website Name:
Date changed:
Email Address:
Username:
Password:
Notes:

K

Website Name:
Date changed:
Email Address:
Username:
Password:
Notes:

Website Name:
Date changed:
Email Address:
Username:
Password:
Notes:

Website Name:
Date changed:
Email Address:
Username:
Password:
Notes:

K

Website Name:
Date changed:
Email Address:
Username:
Password:
Notes:

Website Name:
Date changed:
Email Address:
Username:
Password:
Notes:

Website Name:
Date changed:
Email Address:
Username:
Password:
Notes:

K

Website Name:
Date changed:
Email Address:
Username:
Password:
Notes:

Website Name:
Date changed:
Email Address:
Username:
Password:
Notes:

Website Name:
Date changed:
Email Address:
Username:
Password:
Notes:

K

Website Name:
Date changed:
Email Address:
Username:
Password:
Notes:

Website Name:
Date changed:
Email Address:
Username:
Password:
Notes:

Website Name:
Date changed:
Email Address:
Username:
Password:
Notes:

L

Website Name:
Date changed:
Email Address:
Username:
Password:
Notes:

Website Name:
Date changed:
Email Address:
Username:
Password:
Notes:

Website Name:
Date changed:
Email Address:
Username:
Password:
Notes:

L

Website Name:
Date changed:
Email Address:
Username:
Password:
Notes:

Website Name:
Date changed:
Email Address:
Username:
Password:
Notes:

Website Name:
Date changed:
Email Address:
Username:
Password:
Notes:

L

Website Name:
Date changed:
Email Address:
Username:
Password:
Notes:

Website Name:
Date changed:
Email Address:
Username:
Password:
Notes:

Website Name:
Date changed:
Email Address:
Username:
Password:
Notes:

L

Website Name:
Date changed:
Email Address:
Username:
Password:
Notes:

Website Name:
Date changed:
Email Address:
Username:
Password:
Notes:

Website Name:
Date changed:
Email Address:
Username:
Password:
Notes:

M

Website Name:
Date changed:
Email Address:
Username:
Password:
Notes:

Website Name:
Date changed:
Email Address:
Username:
Password:
Notes:

Website Name:
Date changed:
Email Address:
Username:
Password:
Notes:

M

Website Name:
Date changed:
Email Address:
Username:
Password:
Notes:

Website Name:
Date changed:
Email Address:
Username:
Password:
Notes:

Website Name:
Date changed:
Email Address:
Username:
Password:
Notes:

M

Website Name:
Date changed:
Email Address:
Username:
Password:
Notes:

Website Name:
Date changed:
Email Address:
Username:
Password:
Notes:

Website Name:
Date changed:
Email Address:
Username:
Password:
Notes:

M

Website Name:
Date changed:
Email Address:
Username:
Password:
Notes:

Website Name:
Date changed:
Email Address:
Username:
Password:
Notes:

Website Name:
Date changed:
Email Address:
Username:
Password:
Notes:

N

Website Name:
Date changed:
Email Address:
Username:
Password:
Notes:

Website Name:
Date changed:
Email Address:
Username:
Password:
Notes:

Website Name:
Date changed:
Email Address:
Username:
Password:
Notes:

N

Website Name:
Date changed:
Email Address:
Username:
Password:
Notes:

Website Name:
Date changed:
Email Address:
Username:
Password:
Notes:

Website Name:
Date changed:
Email Address:
Username:
Password:
Notes:

N

Website Name:
Date changed:
Email Address:
Username:
Password:
Notes:

Website Name:
Date changed:
Email Address:
Username:
Password:
Notes:

Website Name:
Date changed:
Email Address:
Username:
Password:
Notes:

N

Website Name:	
Date changed:	
Email Address:	
Username:	
Password:	
Notes:	

Website Name:	
Date changed:	
Email Address:	
Username:	
Password:	
Notes:	

Website Name:	
Date changed:	
Email Address:	
Username:	
Password:	
Notes:	

O

Website Name:
Date changed:
Email Address:
Username:
Password:
Notes:

Website Name:
Date changed:
Email Address:
Username:
Password:
Notes:

Website Name:
Date changed:
Email Address:
Username:
Password:
Notes:

O

Website Name:
Date changed:
Email Address:
Username:
Password:
Notes:

Website Name:
Date changed:
Email Address:
Username:
Password:
Notes:

Website Name:
Date changed:
Email Address:
Username:
Password:
Notes:

O

Website Name:
Date changed:
Email Address:
Username:
Password:
Notes:

Website Name:
Date changed:
Email Address:
Username:
Password:
Notes:

Website Name:
Date changed:
Email Address:
Username:
Password:
Notes:

O

Website Name:
Date changed:
Email Address:
Username:
Password:
Notes:

Website Name:
Date changed:
Email Address:
Username:
Password:
Notes:

Website Name:
Date changed:
Email Address:
Username:
Password:
Notes:

P

Website Name:
Date changed:
Email Address:
Username:
Password:
Notes:

Website Name:
Date changed:
Email Address:
Username:
Password:
Notes:

Website Name:
Date changed:
Email Address:
Username:
Password:
Notes:

P

Website Name:
Date changed:
Email Address:
Username:
Password:
Notes:

Website Name:
Date changed:
Email Address:
Username:
Password:
Notes:

Website Name:
Date changed:
Email Address:
Username:
Password:
Notes:

P

Website Name:
Date changed:
Email Address:
Username:
Password:
Notes:

Website Name:
Date changed:
Email Address:
Username:
Password:
Notes:

Website Name:
Date changed:
Email Address:
Username:
Password:
Notes:

P

Website Name:
Date changed:
Email Address:
Username:
Password:
Notes:

Website Name:
Date changed:
Email Address:
Username:
Password:
Notes:

Website Name:
Date changed:
Email Address:
Username:
Password:
Notes:

Q

Website Name:
Date changed:
Email Address:
Username:
Password:
Notes:

Website Name:
Date changed:
Email Address:
Username:
Password:
Notes:

Website Name:
Date changed:
Email Address:
Username:
Password:
Notes:

Q

Website Name:
Date changed:
Email Address:
Username:
Password:
Notes:

Website Name:
Date changed:
Email Address:
Username:
Password:
Notes:

Website Name:
Date changed:
Email Address:
Username:
Password:
Notes:

Q

Website Name:
Date changed:
Email Address:
Username:
Password:
Notes:

Website Name:
Date changed:
Email Address:
Username:
Password:
Notes:

Website Name:
Date changed:
Email Address:
Username:
Password:
Notes:

Q

Website Name:
Date changed:
Email Address:
Username:
Password:
Notes:

Website Name:
Date changed:
Email Address:
Username:
Password:
Notes:

Website Name:
Date changed:
Email Address:
Username:
Password:
Notes:

R

Website Name:
Date changed:
Email Address:
Username:
Password:
Notes:

Website Name:
Date changed:
Email Address:
Username:
Password:
Notes:

Website Name:
Date changed:
Email Address:
Username:
Password:
Notes:

R

Website Name:
Date changed:
Email Address:
Username:
Password:
Notes:

Website Name:
Date changed:
Email Address:
Username:
Password:
Notes:

Website Name:
Date changed:
Email Address:
Username:
Password:
Notes:

R

Website Name:
Date changed:
Email Address:
Username:
Password:
Notes:

Website Name:
Date changed:
Email Address:
Username:
Password:
Notes:

Website Name:
Date changed:
Email Address:
Username:
Password:
Notes:

R

Website Name:	
Date changed:	
Email Address:	
Username:	
Password:	
Notes:	

Website Name:	
Date changed:	
Email Address:	
Username:	
Password:	
Notes:	

Website Name:	
Date changed:	
Email Address:	
Username:	
Password:	
Notes:	

S

Website Name:
Date changed:
Email Address:
Username:
Password:
Notes:

Website Name:
Date changed:
Email Address:
Username:
Password:
Notes:

Website Name:
Date changed:
Email Address:
Username:
Password:
Notes:

S

Website Name:	
Date changed:	
Email Address:	
Username:	
Password:	
Notes:	

Website Name:	
Date changed:	
Email Address:	
Username:	
Password:	
Notes:	

Website Name:	
Date changed:	
Email Address:	
Username:	
Password:	
Notes:	

S

Website Name:
Date changed:
Email Address:
Username:
Password:
Notes:

Website Name:
Date changed:
Email Address:
Username:
Password:
Notes:

Website Name:
Date changed:
Email Address:
Username:
Password:
Notes:

S

Website Name:
Date changed:
Email Address:
Username:
Password:
Notes:

Website Name:
Date changed:
Email Address:
Username:
Password:
Notes:

Website Name:
Date changed:
Email Address:
Username:
Password:
Notes:

T

Website Name:
Date changed:
Email Address:
Username:
Password:
Notes:

Website Name:
Date changed:
Email Address:
Username:
Password:
Notes:

Website Name:
Date changed:
Email Address:
Username:
Password:
Notes:

T

Website Name:	
Date changed:	
Email Address:	
Username:	
Password:	
Notes:	

Website Name:	
Date changed:	
Email Address:	
Username:	
Password:	
Notes:	

Website Name:	
Date changed:	
Email Address:	
Username:	
Password:	
Notes:	

T

Website Name:
Date changed:
Email Address:
Username:
Password:
Notes:

Website Name:
Date changed:
Email Address:
Username:
Password:
Notes:

Website Name:
Date changed:
Email Address:
Username:
Password:
Notes:

T

Website Name:
Date changed:
Email Address:
Username:
Password:
Notes:

Website Name:
Date changed:
Email Address:
Username:
Password:
Notes:

Website Name:
Date changed:
Email Address:
Username:
Password:
Notes:

T

Website Name:
Date changed:
Email Address:
Username:
Password:
Notes:

Website Name:
Date changed:
Email Address:
Username:
Password:
Notes:

Website Name:
Date changed:
Email Address:
Username:
Password:
Notes:

T

Website Name:
Date changed:
Email Address:
Username:
Password:
Notes:

Website Name:
Date changed:
Email Address:
Username:
Password:
Notes:

Website Name:
Date changed:
Email Address:
Username:
Password:
Notes:

U

Website Name:
Date changed:
Email Address:
Username:
Password:
Notes:

Website Name:
Date changed:
Email Address:
Username:
Password:
Notes:

Website Name:
Date changed:
Email Address:
Username:
Password:
Notes:

U

Website Name:
Date changed:
Email Address:
Username:
Password:
Notes:

Website Name:
Date changed:
Email Address:
Username:
Password:
Notes:

Website Name:
Date changed:
Email Address:
Username:
Password:
Notes:

U

Website Name:
Date changed:
Email Address:
Username:
Password:
Notes:

Website Name:
Date changed:
Email Address:
Username:
Password:
Notes:

Website Name:
Date changed:
Email Address:
Username:
Password:
Notes:

U

Website Name:
Date changed:
Email Address:
Username:
Password:
Notes:

Website Name:
Date changed:
Email Address:
Username:
Password:
Notes:

Website Name:
Date changed:
Email Address:
Username:
Password:
Notes:

V

Website Name:
Date changed:
Email Address:
Username:
Password:
Notes:

Website Name:
Date changed:
Email Address:
Username:
Password:
Notes:

Website Name:
Date changed:
Email Address:
Username:
Password:
Notes:

V

Website Name:
Date changed:
Email Address:
Username:
Password:
Notes:

Website Name:
Date changed:
Email Address:
Username:
Password:
Notes:

Website Name:
Date changed:
Email Address:
Username:
Password:
Notes:

V

Website Name:
Date changed:
Email Address:
Username:
Password:
Notes:

Website Name:
Date changed:
Email Address:
Username:
Password:
Notes:

Website Name:
Date changed:
Email Address:
Username:
Password:
Notes:

V

Website Name:
Date changed:
Email Address:
Username:
Password:
Notes:

Website Name:
Date changed:
Email Address:
Username:
Password:
Notes:

Website Name:
Date changed:
Email Address:
Username:
Password:
Notes:

W

Website Name:
Date changed:
Email Address:
Username:
Password:
Notes:

Website Name:
Date changed:
Email Address:
Username:
Password:
Notes:

Website Name:
Date changed:
Email Address:
Username:
Password:
Notes:

W

Website Name:
Date changed:
Email Address:
Username:
Password:
Notes:

Website Name:
Date changed:
Email Address:
Username:
Password:
Notes:

Website Name:
Date changed:
Email Address:
Username:
Password:
Notes:

W

Website Name:
Date changed:
Email Address:
Username:
Password:
Notes:

Website Name:
Date changed:
Email Address:
Username:
Password:
Notes:

Website Name:
Date changed:
Email Address:
Username:
Password:
Notes:

W

Website Name:
Date changed:
Email Address:
Username:
Password:
Notes:

Website Name:
Date changed:
Email Address:
Username:
Password:
Notes:

Website Name:
Date changed:
Email Address:
Username:
Password:
Notes:

X

Website Name:
Date changed:
Email Address:
Username:
Password:
Notes:

Website Name:
Date changed:
Email Address:
Username:
Password:
Notes:

Website Name:
Date changed:
Email Address:
Username:
Password:
Notes:

X

Website Name:	
Date changed:	
Email Address:	
Username:	
Password:	
Notes:	

Website Name:	
Date changed:	
Email Address:	
Username:	
Password:	
Notes:	

Website Name:	
Date changed:	
Email Address:	
Username:	
Password:	
Notes:	

X

Website Name:
Date changed:
Email Address:
Username:
Password:
Notes:

Website Name:
Date changed:
Email Address:
Username:
Password:
Notes:

Website Name:
Date changed:
Email Address:
Username:
Password:
Notes:

X

Website Name:	
Date changed:	
Email Address:	
Username:	
Password:	
Notes:	

Website Name:	
Date changed:	
Email Address:	
Username:	
Password:	
Notes:	

Website Name:	
Date changed:	
Email Address:	
Username:	
Password:	
Notes:	

Y

Website Name:
Date changed:
Email Address:
Username:
Password:
Notes:

Website Name:
Date changed:
Email Address:
Username:
Password:
Notes:

Website Name:
Date changed:
Email Address:
Username:
Password:
Notes:

Y

Website Name:
Date changed:
Email Address:
Username:
Password:
Notes:

Website Name:
Date changed:
Email Address:
Username:
Password:
Notes:

Website Name:
Date changed:
Email Address:
Username:
Password:
Notes:

Y

Website Name:
Date changed:
Email Address:
Username:
Password:
Notes:

Website Name:
Date changed:
Email Address:
Username:
Password:
Notes:

Website Name:
Date changed:
Email Address:
Username:
Password:
Notes:

Y

Website Name:
Date changed:
Email Address:
Username:
Password:
Notes:

Website Name:
Date changed:
Email Address:
Username:
Password:
Notes:

Website Name:
Date changed:
Email Address:
Username:
Password:
Notes:

Z

Website Name:
Date changed:
Email Address:
Username:
Password:
Notes:

Website Name:
Date changed:
Email Address:
Username:
Password:
Notes:

Website Name:
Date changed:
Email Address:
Username:
Password:
Notes:

Z

Website Name:
Date changed:
Email Address:
Username:
Password:
Notes:

Website Name:
Date changed:
Email Address:
Username:
Password:
Notes:

Website Name:
Date changed:
Email Address:
Username:
Password:
Notes:

Z

Website Name:
Date changed:
Email Address:
Username:
Password:
Notes:

Website Name:
Date changed:
Email Address:
Username:
Password:
Notes:

Website Name:
Date changed:
Email Address:
Username:
Password:
Notes:

Z

Website Name:
Date changed:
Email Address:
Username:
Password:
Notes:

Website Name:
Date changed:
Email Address:
Username:
Password:
Notes:

Website Name:
Date changed:
Email Address:
Username:
Password:
Notes:

ABOUT KYLE KERSKIE

Kye is the co-founder of Privacy-Mentor.com. This website was created as a guide to help you reclaim your privacy in the digital age. Kyle, along with his mother, Carrie Kerskie, an internationally recognized speaker, author and consultant on identity theft and privacy, have helped thousands of victims recover. They wanted to help people BEFORE becoming a victim. The result was...

Privacy-Mentor.com.

To learn more visit Privacy-Mentor.com.